CHECKERBOARD BIOGRAPHY LIBRARY

EXPLORERS

# John
# Smith

Kristin Petrie

Publishing Company

# visit us at
# www.abdopublishing.com

Published by ABDO Publishing Company, 4940 Viking Drive, Edina, Minnesota 55435.
Copyright © 2007 by Abdo Consulting Group, Inc. International copyrights reserved in all
countries. No part of this book may be reproduced in any form without written permission from
the publisher. The Checkerboard Library™ is a trademark and logo of ABDO Publishing
Company.

Printed in the United States.

Cover Photos: North Wind
Interior Photos: Corbis pp. 9, 11, 15; North Wind pp. 5, 7, 13, 17, 19, 21, 23, 25, 29

Series Coordinator: Heidi M. Dahmes
Editors: Heidi M. Dahmes, Megan Murphy
Art Direction & Cover Design: Neil Klinepier
Interior Design & Maps: Dave Bullen

## Library of Congress Cataloging-in-Publication Data

Petrie, Kristin, 1970-
  John Smith / Kristin Petrie.
    p. cm. -- (Explorers)
  Includes index.
  ISBN-10 1-59679-751-7
  ISBN-13 978-1-59679-751-2
  1. Smith, John, 1580-1631--Juvenile literature. 2. Colonists--Virginia--Jamestown--Biography--
Juvenile literature. 3. Explorers--America--Biography--Juvenile literature. 4. Explorers--Great
Britain--Biography--Juvenile literature. 5. Jamestown (Va.)--History--17th century--Juvenile
literature. 6. Jamestown (Va.)--Biography--Juvenile literature. 7. Virginia--History--Colonial
period, ca. 1600-1775--Juvenile literature. I. Title  II. Series: Petrie, Kristin, d 1970- .
Explorers.

F229.S7P48 2006
975.5'02'092--dc22
                                                                        2005017505

# Contents

# Captain Smith

Captain John Smith is recognized as one of the first heroes in the New World.  He saved England's first permanent North American colony, Jamestown, from failure.  When he wasn't saving Jamestown, he was exploring North America's eastern coast.

In addition to these achievements, Smith was a writer and a mapmaker.  But he didn't stop there!   Smith was also a leader, a trader, and an **entrepreneur**.  Amazingly, Smith fulfilled all of these roles after years of battle and travel.

Smith's adventures took him through Europe and North America.  Later in life, he wrote eight books based on his explorations.  Many historians believe he exaggerated details of his voyages.  Still, his tales drew settlers to the New World.  Smith's life parallels the stories of some of the most fearless men in history.

*1271*
Polo left for Asia

*1295*
Polo returned to Italy

*1254*
Marco Polo born

*1275*
Polo met Kublai Khan

THE PORTRAICTUER OF CAPTAYNE JOHN SMITH / ADMIRALL OF NEW ENGLAND

Many Englishmen hoped to find gold and diamonds in North America. But John Smith knew that the real wealth of the continent was in timber, fish, and furs. It took years, but he eventually proved this was true.

**1460 or 1474**
Juan Ponce de León born

**1480**
Ferdinand Magellan born

**1324**
Polo died

**1475**
Vasco Núñez de Balboa born

# Early Life

John Smith was **baptized** on January 6, 1580, in Willoughby, England. His parents were George Smith and Alice Rickards. John had a brother, Francis, and a sister, Alice.

George and Alice were **tenant farmers**. But unlike many tenant farmers, George owned some of his own land. He was also a member of the **gentry**.

Even before his fifth birthday, young John was helping out on the farm. When he was six or seven, he began **grammar school** in nearby Alford. John and his classmates studied the usual subjects of that time. These included English, Latin, Greek, and arithmetic.

When John was nine, his parents sent him to a prominent grammar school in Louth, another nearby town. John's formal schooling ended by the time he was 16.

1500
Balboa joined expedition to South America

1493
Ponce de León joined expedition to New World

1502
Ponce de León became governor of Higüey

In 1588, the English defeated the Spanish Armada. John heard tales of war and travel and was impressed.

Only the wealthiest, brightest students went on to study at a university.  Instead, John became an **apprentice** to a merchant named Thomas Sendall in Lynn, England. However, the apprenticeship bored John.  Then his father died, and everything changed.

# The Travel Bug

When his father died, John inherited land and livestock. But, he was not interested in farming. So, he sold the land and the livestock and used the money to travel. John set off for London, England, and Paris, France.

Over time, John spent all of his money. But he refused to go back to Willoughby. Instead, John decided to volunteer for the French army. He traveled to Le Havre, France, where the army had its headquarters.

Unfortunately, John had no military training. So, he was not suitable for this army. But, John refused to take no for an answer. Impressed by his determination, a French captain sent John to a **mercenary** company. There, Captain Joseph Duxbury welcomed him.

John first experienced battle at the siege of Amiens in 1597. French troops fought to protect the city from Spain's control. For his bravery, John was promoted to sergeant. He also had the opportunity to meet King Henry IV of France.

**1520**
Magellan discovered the Strait of Magellan

**1554**
Walter Raleigh born

**1519**
Magellan led expedition to Spice Islands; Balboa died

**1521**
Ponce de León's third expedition, died in Cuba; Magellan died

Would you have the courage to travel to distant lands by yourself? Do you think Smith ever got homesick?

**Paris fascinated John! He was not used to such grand architecture. Everywhere he turned, he saw inns, theaters, and cathedrals.**

# Rising in Rank

Shortly after the siege of Amiens, the war between France and Spain ended. Sergeant Smith had to look for new work. Spain was trying to gain power over the Dutch. Therefore, Smith traveled to Amsterdam, Netherlands, to offer his services to the Dutch.

Again, the young **mercenary** proved his worth as a soldier. Smith fought bravely against Spain. Later in the war, Smith was seriously wounded. He spent six months recovering. When he returned to the field, Smith was promoted again. He was now an officer!

As winter approached, the Dutch and the Spanish made a peace agreement. The mercenaries were **discharged** from their duties. This meant Smith was out of work again. Most of his fellow mercenaries searched for their next battle. But, Smith needed a break from fighting.

1580
John Smith born

1585
Raleigh knighted by Queen Elizabeth I

1565
Henry Hudson born

1584–1589
Raleigh sponsored expeditions

# THE TRUE TRAVELS, ADVENTVRES,

## AND

## OBSERVATIONS

OF

Captaine IOHN SMITH,

In *Europe, Asia, Affrica,* and *America,* from *Anno Domini* 1593. to 1629.

His Accidents and Sea-fights in the Straights; his Service and Stratagems of warre in *Hungaria, Transilvania, Wallachia,* and *Moldavia,* against the *Turks,* and *Tartars;* his three single combats betwixt the *Christian* Armie and the *Turkes.*

After how he was taken prisoner by the *Turks,* sold for a Slave, sent into *Tartaria;* his description of the *Tartars,* their strange manners and customes of Religions, Diets, Buildings, Warres, Feasts, Ceremonies, and Living; how hee slew the Bashaw of *Nalbrits* in *Cambia,* and escaped from the *Turkes* and *Tartars.*

Together with a continuation of his generall History of *Virginia, Summer-Iles, New England,* and their proceedings, since 1624. to this present 1629; as also of the new Plantations of the great River of the *Amazons,* the Iles of St. *Christopher, Mevis,* and *Barbados* in the *West Indies.*

All written by actuall Authours, whose names you shall finde along the History.

LONDON,

Printed by *J. H.* for *Thomas Slater,* and are to bee sold at the Blew Bible in *Greene Arbour.* 1630.

In 1630, Smith published *The True Travels, Adventures, and Observations of Captain John Smith.* He included many boastful tales from his battle experiences in the book.

# Captured!

Next, Smith lived in Amsterdam for a while. There, he met geographer Peter Plancius. The men discussed travel and exploration. While returning to England, Smith met explorer Henry Hudson. Smith listened eagerly to Hudson's theory about a water passage across North America to Asia.

Smith spent a short time in England. With so many thoughts of adventure, he was restless. So in 1600, he joined the Austrian army and fought fearlessly against the Turks. While fighting in Hungary, Smith was promoted to captain.

In 1602, Captain Smith was wounded in battle and taken prisoner by the Turks. Smith and the other prisoners were sold as slaves. A **pasha** named Timor bought Smith as a present for Lady Charatza Tragabigzanda.

Smith eventually won his new **captor**'s heart. However, this friendship was discovered. Smith was sent back to Timor, who treated him badly. After killing his cruel owner, Smith escaped. He returned to England in 1604.

*1595*
Raleigh led first expedition

*1588*
Raleigh helped defeat the Spanish Armada

*1606*
Smith joined expedition to North America

# Would You?

Would you be brave enough to make friends with your enemy? Do you think Smith hoped to escape by making friends with his captor?

The Turks were part of the Ottoman Empire. During the 1600s, this empire covered parts of Eastern Europe, the Middle East, and North Africa.

# The New World

Back in England, Smith got involved in planning a North American expedition.  Spain was becoming wealthy from riches found in new lands.  King James I of England hoped to have the same luck in North America.

On December 20, 1606, Smith departed from London for the area known as Virginia.  This was North America's entire east coast north of Florida.  About 105 men boarded three ships prepared for the journey.  Smith sailed on the *Susan Constant.*

There were several purposes for the expedition.  The settlers were to establish a colony, as well as search for gold and silver.  Last, they were to seek a waterway connecting the Atlantic and Pacific oceans.  Each goal they accomplished would increase England's trading opportunities and wealth.

On April 26, 1607, the settlers reached Chesapeake Bay.  There, they opened a sealed box.  It contained the names of

1607
Hudson's first expedition

1609
Hudson's third expedition

1608
Hudson's second expedition

The *Susan Constant*, the *Godspeed*, and the *Discovery* delivered the first settlers to Jamestown. You can view these models at Jamestown Settlement in Virginia.

those who had been appointed to the governing council for the new colony. Six noblemen and Smith were on that list.

The other leaders did not like Smith. So, they refused to let him sit on the council. Smith did not fight with the men. He had more important things on his mind. He began exploring.

*1614*
Smith led expedition to North America, charted and named New England

*1610–1611*
Hudson's last expedition, he died

*1616*
Raleigh's second expedition

# Jamestown

Smith and a small party ventured up the James River in a shallow boat. They met and spent time with natives. From them, Smith learned that North America was vast, rather than a narrow strip of land. He also concluded that the James River was not a passage to the Pacific Ocean. Farther upstream, the river narrowed.

Smith's party returned to Chesapeake Bay. The **fleet** then sailed up the James River, looking for a suitable settlement site. The ships eventually landed near present-day Williamsburg, Virginia.

On May 14, 1607, the colonists began building their settlement. The primitive town had a fort, houses, and a meeting hall. The settlers named the colony Jamestown, after King James.

Life in the colony was difficult. Natives attacked often, and there was never enough food. Smith taught the settlers how to use muskets for protection and for hunting.

1618
Raleigh died

1637
Jacques Marquette born

1645
Louis Jolliet born

1631
Smith died

1643
René-Robert Cavelier de La Salle born

On May 21, Smith and a small party set out to explore the surrounding rivers. During their travels, they made peace with several tribes and traded for food. Smith became especially interested in maple syrup and blueberries!

**Today, you can visit the site in Virginia where the original Jamestown Colony was located.**

When Smith returned to Jamestown, the settlement was in **chaos**. Natives had attacked the unarmed settlers while they farmed.

Despite opposition, Smith took control of Jamestown's defenses. Under his leadership, the fort was strengthened. And, armed guards were put in place to watch over the settlement. Because of Smith's firm guidance, the settlers survived many **raids**. Finally, Smith was allowed to join the council.

Smith enforced rigid working orders. All of the colonists had to provide for one another. Many of the settlers were unaccustomed to hard labor. However, if someone chose not to work, he did not eat. Jamestown began to improve under Smith's leadership.

Despite Smith's efforts, it took a long time for the colony to provide for itself. Smith traded repeatedly with the natives for food. Without his strong leadership, Jamestown would have been lost.

Smith also continued to explore. He took careful notes about good places for farming and settlement. And he

*1669*
La Salle explored Ohio region

*1666*
La Salle sailed to Canada

*1673*
Marquette and Jolliet explored the Mississippi River

The Jamestown colonists endured many attacks by natives.

created detailed, **accurate** maps.  In time, Smith put his writings and maps into several books.

Smith discovered that peace with the natives was not always possible.  During one journey, natives captured Smith.  Then, they took him to their leader, who was known as Powhatan.  In later writings, Smith claims that Powhatan ordered his execution.   But, Powhatan's young daughter Pocahontas saved him!

# More Travels

Many believe the Pocahontas story is untrue. But somehow, Smith returned to Jamestown in January 1608. Once again the settlement was in disorder. More colonists had arrived. And, the desire for wealth had taken over.

The new settlers **rebelled** against Smith. But not for long. Smith told them that they were free to go search for gold. However, they would not be welcome to come back. There were many dangers outside of the settlement's walls. So for most, it was not a tough decision to make.

Peace was temporarily restored. Sadly, agreement among the settlers never lasted long. Smith may have become frustrated, because he left Jamestown yet again.

In summer 1608, Smith set out on another voyage. He explored the region surrounding Chesapeake Bay. On this journey, Smith discovered the mouth of the Potomac River.

1675
Marquette died

1682
La Salle's second Mississippi River expedition

1679
La Salle's first Mississippi River expedition

# Would You?

Would you enjoy ruling a new settlement? Would you know what type of buildings were needed? How do you think Smith made peace with the natives?

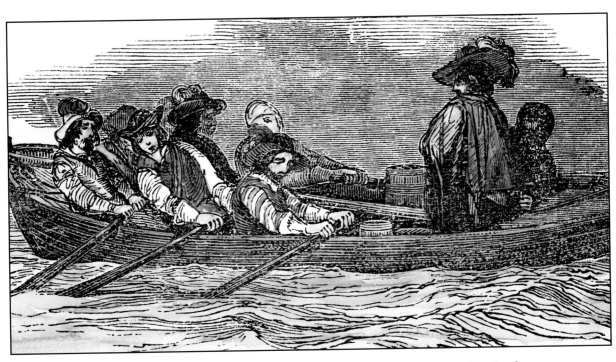

**Smith seemed to have endless energy! He never tired of exploring, even after all the work he did for the colony.**

*1687*
La Salle died

*1684*
La Salle's third Mississippi River expedition

*1700*
Jolliet died

With only a compass, he continued to make amazingly **accurate** maps. Smith's descriptions of the region are thorough and appealing.

In June, Smith's party sailed up the Potomac. The explorers hoped it was the passage to the Pacific Ocean. They had a great time fishing. Unfortunately, their fun ended when a fish stung Smith and another man broke his leg.

These accidents put an end to the exploring. The team headed back to Jamestown. Yet again, Smith faced **chaos**. This time, problems arose when the new settlers became ill from the heat. Others were angry with the colony's president. He had demanded they build him a large home.

The settlers quickly approached Smith with their problems. They insisted he take over the position of president. Smith became president on September 10, 1608.

At this point, Smith wasn't very interested in politics. He wanted adventure! So, he hired a trusted friend to oversee the colony's affairs. Three days after the election, Smith left for the wilderness again. He mapped more of the Chesapeake Bay area.

*1770*
William Clark born

*1786*
Sacagawea born

*1774*
Meriwether Lewis born

*1800*
Sacagawea captured

# A TRVE RELation of such occur-

rences and accidents of noate as hath hapned in Virginia since the first planting of that Collony, which is now resident in the South part thereof, till the last returne from thence.

*Written by Captaine* Smith *one of the said Collony, to a worshipfull friend of his in England.*

LONDON

Printed for *John Tappe*, and are to bee solde at the Grey-hound in Paules-Church-yard, by *W. W.*

1 6 0 8

In 1608, Smith published *A True Relation*. This book contains descriptions of life in Jamestown.

# Growing Colony

When Smith returned to Jamestown, the colony began to prosper under his rule.  Finally, Jamestown's crops began to flourish.  The settlers could now provide food for themselves.  Smith also oversaw the construction of new houses, warehouses, and a better fort.  The fort's star shape became the standard throughout future British colonies.

In fall 1608, the first female settlers arrived at Jamestown.  They were Mistress Forrest and her maid, Anne Burras.  With their arrival, the town started to resemble a more civilized place.  The men began thinking of Jamestown as a permanent settlement.  Soon, more women arrived.

After governing the growing colony every day, Smith was exhausted.  Nevertheless, he spent long hours working on his next book.  In *A Map of Virginia with a Description of the Country*, Smith continues his report on life in Jamestown.

1804
Lewis and Clark began exploring the Pacific Northwest

1806
Lewis and Clark returned to Missouri

1805
Sacagawea joined the Lewis and Clark expedition

**During Smith's time as president, no settlers died of starvation.**

Smith's time in Jamestown drew to a close in September 1609. An accidental fire in his gunpowder bag severely burned him. He sailed back to England for proper medical care. Jamestown's best leader never returned to the colony.

*1812*
Sacagawea died

*1856*
Robert Edwin Peary born

*1809*
Lewis died

*1838*
Clark died

*1881*
Peary entered the U.S. Navy

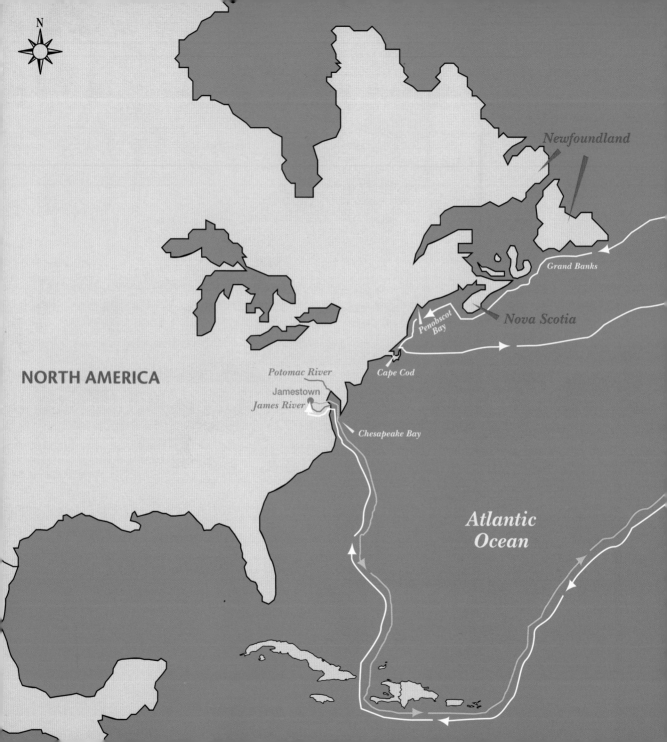

N

NORTH AMERICA

*Newfoundland*

*Grand Banks*

*Nova Scotia*

*Penobscot Bay*

*Potomac River*

Jamestown

*James River*

*Cape Cod*

*Chesapeake Bay*

*Atlantic Ocean*

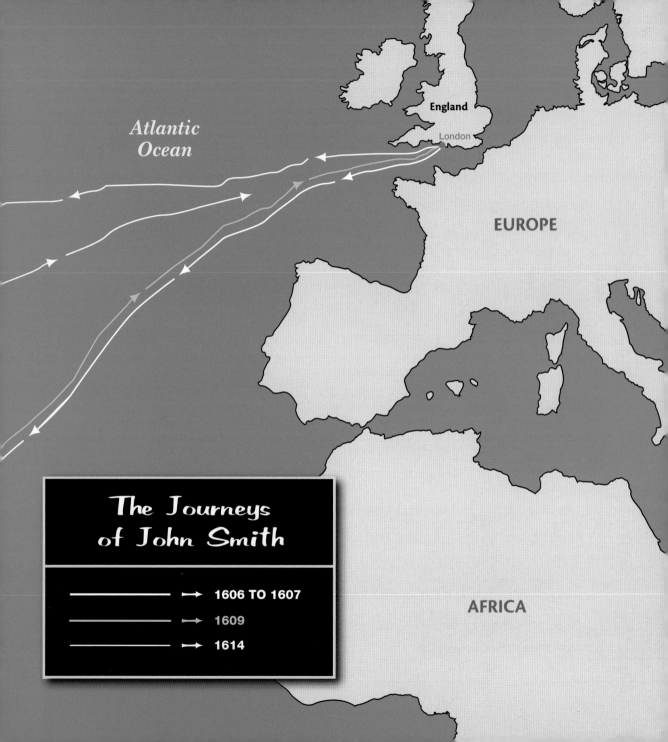

# Last Years

Smith had been a respected leader in the New World. But to the king and to the expedition's investors, Smith and Jamestown were failures. The Jamestown settlers had not sent gold and silver back to England. And, the colonists had failed to find a passage to the Pacific Ocean.

Smith spent months recovering in a small house near the Thames River. Overcome by **depression**, he thought only of returning to the New World.

In 1614, Smith again set sail for North America. This time, his small **fleet** reached the Grand Banks of Newfoundland and then present-day Nova Scotia. Continuing south, Smith mapped the North American coast from Penobscot Bay to Cape Cod. He named the area New England.

Smith returned to England with large stocks of fish oil, fish, and furs. The expedition's investors profited greatly. Smith led another voyage the next year. But that time, pirates captured him and held him prisoner for three months.

*1893*
Peary's first expedition

*1909*
Peary's third expedition, reached the North Pole

*1905*
Peary's second expedition

*1920*
Peary died

Then in 1617, he planned one last expedition to colonize New England. But, bad weather prevented him from sailing.

Smith's New World discoveries made him famous. And, his writings drew new settlers to the area. Captain John Smith continued to write until his death on June 21, 1631.

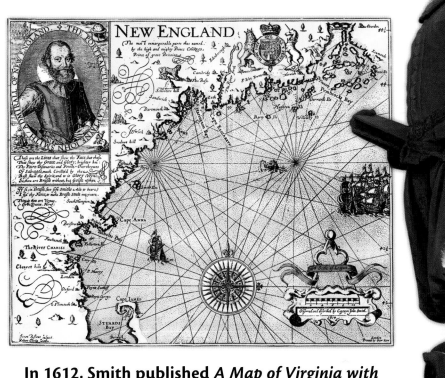

**In 1612, Smith published *A Map of Virginia with a Description of the Country*. This book includes the maps from his summer 1608 explorations.**

# Glossary

**accurate** - free of errors.  Something with errors is inaccurate.

**apprentice** - a person who learns a trade or a craft from a skilled worker.

**baptize** - to be admitted into the Christian community during a ceremony involving the ritual use of water.

**captor** - one who has captured a person or a thing.

**chaos** - a state of total confusion.

**depression** - a state of feeling sad and dejected.

**discharge** - to release from military service.

**entrepreneur** - one who organizes, manages, and accepts the risks of a business or an enterprise.

**fleet** - a group of ships under one command.

**gentry** - a class ranking below the nobility.

**grammar school** - a school including usually the first four to the first eight grades and often a kindergarten.

**mercenary** - a soldier serving in a foreign army for pay.

**pasha** - a man of high rank or office in Turkey or in northern Africa.

**raid** - a sudden attack.

**rebel** - to disobey an authority or the government.  One who participates in acts of disobedience or armed resistance is a rebel.

**tenant farmer** - a farmer who works land owned by another and pays rent either in cash or in shares of produce.

# Saying It

**Amiens** - awm-YEHN
**entrepreneur** - ahn-truh-pruh-NUHR
**Le Havre** - luh HAHVRUH
**Louth** - LAUTH
**Newfoundland** - NOO-fuhnd-luhnd
**Penobscot Bay** - puh-NAHB-skuht BAY
**Potomac** - puh-TOH-muhk
**Powhatan** - pau-uh-TAN
**Thames** - TEHMZ

# Web Sites

To learn more about John Smith, visit ABDO Publishing Company on the World Wide Web at **www.abdopublishing.com**. Web sites about Smith are featured on our Book Links page. These links are routinely monitored and updated to provide the most current information available.

# Index